# KENT *in* WINTER

ANDREAS BYRNE

HALSGROVE

First published in Great Britain in 2010

Title page photograph:
**Fairfield Church Dawn.**
Frosty dawn over Fairfield church as the sheep wait for the sun to rise and melt the ice.

British Library Cataloguing-in-Publication Data
A CIP record for this title is available from the British Library

ISBN 978 0 85704 052 7

**HALSGROVE**
Halsgrove House,
Ryelands Industrial Estate,
Bagley Road, Wellington, Somerset TA21 9PZ
Tel: 01823 653777    Fax: 01823 216796
email: sales@halsgrove.com

Part of the Halsgrove group of companies
Information on all Halsgrove titles is available at: www.halsgrove.com

Printed and bound in Italy by Grafiche Flaminia

# INTRODUCTION

This book is divided by three seasons, starting from late autumn through to the main season of winter and just into spring.

It was early December 2009 and I was sitting in the conservatory having a cup of coffee, looking out into the garden and thinking to myself that I need a project. Lo and behold a call comes through offering me an opportunity to do another book, this time set in winter and in Kent. Fantastic I thought, I had a few stock photos of snowy Kent but I needed more, a lot more! Fate smiled on me because within a week it snowed, magically transforming Kent into 'A Winter's Wonderland' … Yes it was all my fault!

From a photographer's point of view snow is a beautiful thing as it changes the landscape from the ordinary to the extraordinary and motivated me into capturing wonderful scenes in Kent. The trouble starts when you want to get out and photograph it! Some minor roads become impassable as the snow wasn't cleared and other major routes become jammed due to accidents and general travel chaos! So I decided to stay local in my first forays and I was surprised at the wonderful landscapes to be had on my doorstep: Broadditch Pond is less that a mile away and yet I had never photographed it! Armed with Wellington boots, coats, gloves, hat, camera, tripod and a shovel I ventured forth into the white blue yonder!

Sun, snow and bright blue skies are the ingredients for beautiful winter pictures and in this first week the weather followed this pattern so I was lucky and able to take lots of shots in this winter week. The snow had gone by Christmas so I was able to get out and about more easily and concentrated on getting some festive lights. Bluewater shopping centre was lit up like a Christmas tree and proved to be a good source as did Canterbury Cathedral with a life sized Nativity scene standing just outside and Christmas carols hanging in the night air whilst I took the photos, very festive!

Wildlife becomes slightly more approachable during the harsh days of winter as animals and birds need to stock up on available food sources, making the garden a good place to photograph them feasting on various berries and feeders.

The winter of 2009-2010 proved to be a long and cold one, with freezing temperatures, ice, snow, frost, arctic winds, fog and rain, a real seasonal mix of weather which I have tried to capture through my camera. It was only by mid March that the temperatures rose back into double figures and spring began to emerge from its thawing slumber. And so ends my photographic journey, time to put away the thermals, heavy coats and Wellingtons and enjoy the new shoots of spring. The book comes to an end with images of spring flowers, bursting buds, croaking frogs and longer sunny days.

Andreas Byrne, 2010

**Beech Trees.**
Beech trees blaze with autumn colour in a wood near Ide Hill.


*Right:* **Eynsford in Autumn.**
The charming village of Eynsford reflected in the River Darent on a still autumn morning.
Motorists can chose to drive over the bridge or through the ford.

**Fly Agaric Toadstools.**
For a few of weeks in autumn, Beacon Wood Country Park is transformed into fairy land with the emergence of the fly agaric toadstools under the silver birch trees.

*Right:* **Horsmonden Church, Autumn.**
Nestling in the Weald of Kent, Horsmonden church and the oast houses make an iconic composition in the landscape.

**River Eden.**
Oak leaves turning from green to gold along the River Eden near Chiddingstone.


***Left:*** **Crockham Hill.**
Fallen beech leaves carpet the woodland floor with bronze and copper colours.

**Web Site.**
Spiders spin their dew-spangled webs to catch sleepy insects on a misty autumn morning.


*Right:* **Moored Pleasure Boats.**
Boats getting ready for the winter moorings on the River Medway near Yalding.

**Leaves in a Stream.**
Fallen maple leaves rest on a rock in a Kentish stream.


*Right:* **Frozen Pond.**
Reeds stand stiff and white in the early morning frost around
the fishing lakes at Shorne Country Park.

**Trees and Ferns.**
Copper-coloured ferns surround
the silver birch trees in a
Kentish woodland.

**Toys Hill.**
The last golden display before autumn turns to winter.


***Right:*** **Trottiscliffe Church.**
The church nestles in the foothills of the North Downs seen
from Vigo village in the early morning.

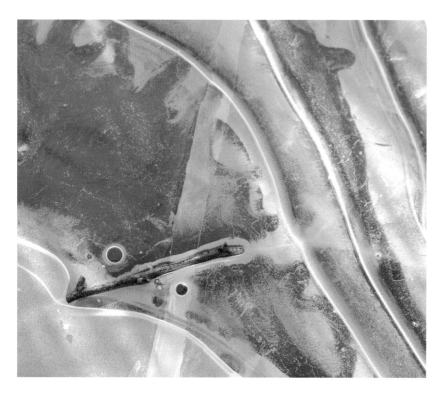

**Ice Patterns.**
Frozen ponds and puddles are transformed into works of art.


*Right:* **Fairfield Church.**
Fairfield church sits cold and isolated surrounded
by frozen dykes in Romney Marsh.

**Frosty Field.**
Frozen crops not yet thawed by the sun's rays near Fairseat.


*Left:* **Fairfield Church.**
The sun gets to work on melting the frost lighting up the church and the surrounding marsh.

**Nurstead Church.**
A sharp frost turns the grass white and is crisp and crunchy underfoot.

**Frosty Trees.**
A frosty tree-fringed field near Meopham as the sun starts to burn off the morning mist.

**Oast House.**
The early morning winter sun bathes the oasts in a warm light off Nurstead Church Lane.

**Nurstead Church.**
A frosty hedgerow of brambles and wild clematis frames Nurstead church and the oasts.

**Misty Sunrise.**
The early morning sun breaks through the mists and glistens on
the morning dew on the North Downs near Wrotham Hill.

*Right:* Wrecked Barge.
A disused decaying barge sits high and dry above
the marshes at Rainham Creek.

**Bewlwater.**
The boat cruises at Bewlwater Reservoir, the largest inland water in the
south east have now come to an end until the spring months.

**Farm House.**
Morning reflections in a flooded field after a wet night on Romney Marsh near Old Romney.

**Minster Bay**.
A huge expanse of mud is revealed at low tide on the Swale Estuary, ideal for visiting seabirds.


*Right:* Swan Lake.
A swan glides effortlessly on the rosy waters at sunrise near the Grove Ferry Inn, Stodmarsh.

**Aylesford.**
The village of Aylesford wakens to a dusting of
snow on the rooftops of the houses.

*Right:* **Aylesford and River.**
The five-arched bridge at Aylseford that spans the
River Medway dates from Roman times and is unsuitable
for modern traffic which crosses on a Bailey bridge
a little further down.

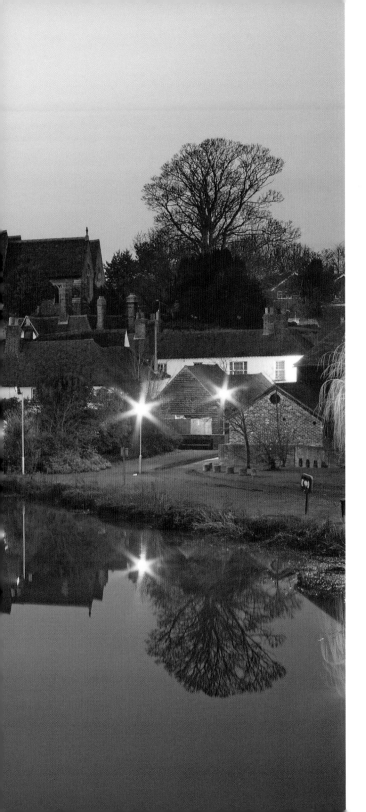

**Snowy Lane, Ash.**
Overnight thick snow arrives in Kent holding
the countryside in its bleak grip at Ash.

*Left:* **Aylesford Reflections.**
A high tide on the River Medway reflects the
village of Aylesford on a calm winter's evening.

**Berry's Maple.**
A distant view out over the snowfields towards Berry's Maple on a cold, gloomy afternoon in winter.

**A Winter's Sky.**
Dispersing snow clouds over the white wilderness of the Gallops as the sun sinks beneath the horizon at Longfield.

**Redwing.**
One of the many winter visitors to the garden
is the Redwing seen here perched on a fir tree.

**Blackbird.**
Blackbirds also like berries – this one is
feeding on holly during a snow shower.

*Left:* **Longfield Lights.**
A gap in the hedgerow reveals Longfield village
at lighting up time from 'the Gallops'.

**Foggy Ash Trees.**
Camer Park takes on a still, mysterious and eerie atmosphere on a cold foggy day.

*Left:* Lone Yacht.
A lone yacht reflected in the water sits motionless at Oare in the hazy afternoon sun.

**Bluewater.**
The largest shopping centre in Europe takes on a festive air with thousands
of Christmas lights illuminating the lakes and shops.

**Bluewater Carousel.**
All the fun of the fair at Christmas time as Bluewater becomes a winter wonderland.

**Rising Sun.**
The pub at Fawkham Green offers a warm inviting refuge from the bitter winter's evening.

**Canterbury Cathedral.**
A Christmas tree stands outside the magnificent illuminated cathedral as the winter moon rises.

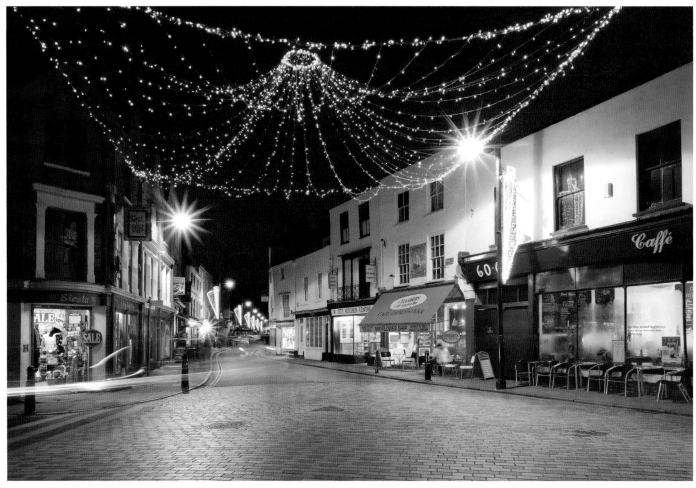

**Palace Street, Canterbury**.
Christmas lights over Palace Street bring festive good cheer to all who visit the city.


*Right:* **Sunset over the River**.
A watery winter's sun sets over the medieval buildings lining the River Stour at Canterbury.

**Robin.**
Every robin needs a snow scene to show him at his best.
This one was sitting amongst the brambles near Yalding.

*Right:* **Reflected Oasts.**
As the snow begins to melt, these iconic oasts are reflected
in the River Medway at Yalding.

**Oast House and Tow Path.**
The tow path that follows the River Medway is a public footpath that leads
the walker towards Yalding village from East Peckham.

**Sunburst.**
The sun breaks through the snow clouds revealing the glassy gritted road as it passes Broadditch Farm Pond.

**Broadditch Pond.**
Framed by wintry trees the half-frozen pond mirrors the willows and sky.

**Snowy Footpath.**
The path through the gate leads through the woods towards Northfleet Green.

**Gateway
to the Woods.**
Snow clouds gather
over the gateway into
the woods as the last
rays of the sun fade
behind a winter's sky.

**Sunset over Camber.**
As the sun sets over Camber Sands the ripples glisten in the low evening light.

**Snow Stile.**
A snowy vista across the fields towards Ridley.

*Left:* **Trees and Snow.**
An arch of beech trees forms a tunnel of snow-covered branches on the footpath through the woods on Wrotham Hill.

**Sunset and Stones.**
Shimmering sands lit by the
setting sun as the water flows
out to sea near Botany Bay.

*Right:* Sheerness Clouds.
The north winds blow
in from the sea bringing
snow clouds over the beach
at Sheerness on the
Isle of Sheppey.

**'Minty'.**
A winter coat comes in handy when the weather is so cold as Minty waits for his breakfast.


*Left:* **Sunset over the Beach and Cliffs.**
As the tide comes in the rock pools begin to fill and reflect the low winter sun near Kingsgate.

**Three Trees.**
As the snow melts the trees cast long shadows in the ploughed field and the
landscape takes on a monochrome appearance near Luddesdown.

**Luddesdown Church.**

A clear blue sky and bright sunshine slowly start to thaw the frozen snow around Luddesdown church.

**Luddesdown Court Farm.**
Cows have to be kept indoors during the wintertime, bedded with straw and fed on silage.

**Knole House.**

Knole House, Sevenoaks is managed by the National Trust.  It was built by Thomas Bourchier,
Archbishop of Canterbury and dates from 1456.

**Deer in Snow.**
Knole House is set in the only remaining medieval deer park in Kent.
The public have free access to the park from Sevenoaks.

**Sunset Through Trees, Knole.**
Skeletal trees silhouetted against the setting sun at Knole Park.

**Brenchley Butcher's Shop.**
Snow creates a Christmas-card scene in the charming village of Brenchley.

**Terry's Butcher's Shop.**
Viewed from the other side of the road the attractive traditional
Kentish-style timbered building gleams in the wintry sun.

*Left:* **Brenchley Church.**
The graveyard and church with a fresh covering of snow.

**Parakeet.**
An unusual vibrant green visitor to the garden attracted by the seed feeders.
Parakeets are becoming more common in the south east and London.

**Snowy Rose.**
Petals frozen in time, a rose blooms in a graveyard at Cobham.

**Crab Apples.**
A large number of fruits are grown in Kent including
crab apples, seen here in snowy rows.


*Right:* **Cobham Church from Fields.**
A distant picture of Cobham church from the snowfields
with the wind breaks surrounding the orchard being
used as a lead-in for the eye to follow.

**St Mary Magdalene Church.**
The snowy public footpath runs by the side of the
church and leads out to the fields at Cobham.

*Right:* Graveyard.
The snow-covered graveyard at the back of
Cobham church makes a picturesque scene.

**Snow Stile.**
A wintry stile leads the walker on through snowfields and orchards around Cobham.

**Number 45.**
A festive front door and letter box on The Street which is the main road through Cobham village.

**Cobham Village Store.**
The village store is one of the oldest buildings in the village dating from
1411 and sells a variety of goods as well as being a tea room.

**Cobham Church and The Street.**
Cobham church has the finest collection of medieval brasses in the world,
some of which are more than 600 years old.

**The Leather Bottle.**
The Leather Bottle was a favourite haunt of Charles Dickens and is important in his novel *The Pickwick Papers*.


*Right:* **Lodge Farm and Dovecote.**
Along Lodge Lane, Cobham a large Victorian dovecote can be seen at Lodge Farm.

**The Lodge House.**
Further along the lane the thatched lodge house sits by a footpath that leads to the Mausoleum
that belonged to Lord Darnley, now fully restored by the National Trust.

**Driveway to Mausoleum.**
One of the several avenues that radiated from Cobham Hall leading to the Mausoleum.

**Lavender Fields.**
Lines of snow-covered lavender lead towards Castle Farm at Lullingstone.

**Eynsford and Melting Snow.**
The Plough pub at Eynsford sits beside a swollen River Darent, which is a popular paddling spot during the summertime.

**Melting Snow, Heaverham.**
Thawing snow surrounds a traditional oast house and cottage on Heaverham Road.

**Foggy Oak Tree.**
Grey freezing fog hangs over a deserted Camer Park with the
occasional hardy dog walker emerging from the mists.

*Left:* **Royal Mail, Kemsing.**
A valiant postman drives through the wintry country lanes delivering his mail.

**Icicles.**
'When icicles hang by the wall…' Echoes of
William Shakspeare. These icicles were hanging from Broadditch
Farm shop, near Southfleet.


*Left:* **Southfleet Village.**
The village starts to warm up in the sunshine after a
cold and wintry night left a fresh covering of snow.

**Manor Farm Barn.**
The glowing willows by the pub add intense colours to this wintry scene.

**Geese in Snow.**
The sun filters through the golden willows on to the geese waiting patiently for food by Broadditch Pond.

**Cherry Orchard.**
A frozen cherry orchard and barn wait for a fruitful summer.

**Apple Orchard.**
Rows of apple trees in the snow near Betsham wait
for the snow to melt before blossoming in April.

**Snowfields, Bean.**
A blanket of snow covers the landscape near the village of Bean.

**Matfield Pond.**
A large willow tree, branches covered with snow, grows on an island
in the middle of the frozen pond at Matfield village.


*Left:* **Tree Branches.**
A magnificent beech tree holds out its arms to the snow.

**Matfield Pond and House.**
In the bright mid-winter Matfield Pond is frozen hard as stone.

**Castle Hill.**
Time to dust off the sledges and snowboards for the chance to enjoy the winter
sports at Castle Hill, not too far from Horsmonden.

**Snowfields.**
Snowy furrowed fields lead towards Upper Bush near Cuxton.

*Left:* **Horsmonden Church.**
Wedding bells were ringing out as I took this picture of
Horsmonden church, after negotiating slippery frozen lanes.

**Meopham Windmill.**
A snowman enjoying the view of the windmill from Meopham Green.

**Nurstead Church.**
Overnight snow has transformed this landscape into a Christmas-card scene.

**Thawing Snowfield.**
Brief spells of sunshine manage to thaw the
hedgerows before everything re-freezes again.

*Left:* **Nurstead Church.**
A distant view of the church, oast house and Nurstead Court.

**Melting Snow, Ash.**
A field of winter crops emerges through the melting snow
revealing the footpath up to Ash Woods.

*Right:* **Horses at Nurstead Court.**
Horses manage to find some green grass to eat
on the frozen ground.

**Nurstead Court.**
A frosty scene looking towards Nurstead Court.

**Frosty Footpath.**
A sun-dappled frozen bridleway leading off the road towards Sallows Shaw.

**Catkins.**
Golden catkins capped with snow on the hazel trees.

*Left:* **Meopham Green and Frost.**
A harsh overnight frost begins to slowly melt
as the sun gets to work on the Green.

**East Wear Bay.**
Winter browns of coastal vegetation clothe the cliffs near Folkestone.

*Right:* Sunset over Oare.
Oare Marshes is an important habitat for wetland birds and is managed by the RSPB.

**Tilbury Power Station.**
Viewed from across the marshes at Chalk, Tilbury Power Station takes
on a new look in the rosy hues of a winter twilight.

*Right:* **Sunset over the Sea.**
Menacing black snow clouds gather, ready to deposit another covering of snow near Tankerton.

**Archbishop's Palace.**
The Archbishop's Palace sits beside the River Medway at Maidstone. The palace was built in the fourteenth century for the Archbishops of Canterbury and is now managed by Kent County Council.

**Mote Park.**
The Earl of Romney Memorial stands overlooking Mote Park with Mote House in the background. The memorial was erected in 1801 by the volunteers of Kent as a tribute to the Lord Lieutenant, the Earl of Romney.

**Geese.**
Geese and other wildfowl on the lake at Haysden Park, near
Tonbridge, take great interest in my cheese sandwich!

*Right:* Tonbridge Castle.
The warm yellow stone of Tonbridge Castle has been standing
since the Normans built it. The Motte and Bailey castle overlooks
the River Medway in the heart of Tonbridge.

**The Flying Horse.**
The pub stands in front of the parish church at Smarden
and is a popular spot in the summertime.

*Right:* Oast Houses, Smarden.
A public footpath leads away from the village of Smarden
on a bright crisp snow-free day in February.

**Biddenden.**
A picture of the high street in the pretty village of
Biddenden, famous for its Siamese twins, (the Biddenden
Maids) who lived here in the twelfth century.

*Left:* **Tree Reflections.**
After heavy rain and snow melt this pond reflects
the skeletal trees of winter in the late afternoon.

**Holden Farm Barn.**
Late afternoon sun brings a warming glow to these oasts at Holden Farm, Three Chimneys.

*Right:* **Cranbrook Windmill.**
The large white Union Windmill at Cranbrook is the finest smock mill in Kent and overlooks the market town. Cranbrook is also known as the capital of the Weald and was a centre of the medieval cloth industry.

A late afternoon reflection in the pond at
Goudhurst of Burfields House.

**Snowdrop.**
A close-up of a snowdrop heralds the ending of winter
and the start of a new season.

**Bee in Crocus.**
The bees don't waste any time and
get going as soon as it's warm
enough to start gathering nectar.

*Right:* **Melliker Farm.**
Frost on a cold morning from the footpath
that goes by Mellikers Farm near Meopham.

**Swans and Oasts.**
Early spring and two swans swim by Fulling Mill Farm near Maidstone.

**Beach Huts.**
A very cold windy day by the sea as the afternoon sun sinks, the last rays
hitting the beach huts overlooking the sea near Seasalter.

**Willow Tree.**
A skeletal willow tree growing out of the windy reeds on the South Swale marshes.

**Whitstable Oysters.**
Empty oyster shells are collected outside the restaurant and recycled for reef restoration.

**Rowing Boat.**
The Whitstable Oyster Company rowing boat rests on the shingle outside the restaurant on a bright cold afternoon.

**Reeds and Dyke.**
The marshes at South Swale are fertile grazing grounds for sheep and
ponies as well as being an ideal habitat for wading birds.

**Horses in Field.**
Bright winter sunshine breaks through the clouds casting long shadows across the field.

*Right:* **Rolvenden Windmill.**
The windmill stands on top of a hill over-looking pastures which will soon be filled with spring lambs.

**Rough with the Smooth.**
Melt water swells the rivers rushing over stones and
creating interesting patterns.

*Left:* **Mote Park Lake.**
Winter willows provide an early
splash of colour around the lake.

**Caramel Wave.**
The sun catches a falling wave looking like molten caramel at Sandwich Bay.

**Rowing Boat.**
A boat all wrapped up in the warm evening winter sun near Camber Sands.


*Right:* **Ash Cricket Club.**
The morning mists of March begin to lift over the cricket ground as the spring sun climbs higher into the sky.

**Frogs.**
The croaking frogs emerge from their winter's rest and
gather for a mass spawning during March.

*Left:* **Leeds Castle.**
'A host of golden daffodils' burst out around
the moat at Leeds Castle, near Maidstone.

**Bluebells.**
Spring flowers carpet the woodland floor before the tree canopy closes
in over them, filling the air with their heady perfume.